JOSEPH GOEBBELS

THE HOLOCAUST™

JOSEPH GOEBBELS

KELLY ROSCOE
AND JEREMY ROBERTS

ROSEN PUBLISHING

Published in 2016 by The Rosen Publishing Group, Inc.
29 East 21st Street, New York, NY 10010

First Edition

Library of Congress Cataloging-in-Publication Data

Roscoe, Kelly.
Joseph Goebbels / Kelly Roscoe and Jeremy Roberts. -- First edition.
pages cm. -- (The Holocaust)
Includes index.
Audience: Grades 7-12.
ISBN 978-1-5081-7049-5 (library bound)
1. Goebbels, Joseph, 1897-1945--Juvenile literature. 2. Nazis--Biography--Juvenile literature. 3. Germany--Politics and government--1933-1945--Juvenile literature. 4. Antisemitism--Germany--History--20th century--Juvenile literature. 5. Propaganda, German--History--20th century--Juvenile literature. I. Roberts, Jeremy, 1956- II. Title.
DD247.G6R67 2015
943.086092--dc23
[B]

2015019515

Manufactured in China

CONTENTS

INTRODUCTION

As the Minister for Propaganda and Culture in Nazi Germany, Joseph Goebbels was one of Adolf Hitler's closest advisers, a man who shared his leader's desire to expel the Jews from Germany by any means necessary, even mass murder. Through his control of radio, film, newspapers, and all other media, he convinced the German people that the Jews were their enemy and that the Nazi Party would return the nation to its former greatness after its humiliating defeat in World War I. Although Goebbels never personally killed a single Jew (as far as historians know), his actions were instrumental to the Holocaust and the death of millions of people.

Furthermore, long before the Nazis set up concentration camps, Goebbels had been one of the key players in Hitler's rise to power. Without him, the Nazis might not have been able to rule Germany so effectively. Goebbels acted as the Party's campaign manager, helping the Nazis win a large enough share of the vote that Hitler was offered the position of chancellor in 1933.

Despite being one of the most powerful and influential people in the Third Reich, Goebbels did not look like a very intimidating person. He stood only five feet tall and weighed roughly one hundred pounds. He was also disabled, with a clubfoot and one leg shorter than the other. He wore a brace and dragged his foot when he walked.

Goebbels' powerful speeches helped convince the public to believe in and fight for the Nazi cause.

However, his greatest skill was as an intensely persuasive public speaker, able to use words and emotions to sway an audience whether speaking to one person or hundreds of thousands. His Ministry of Propaganda produced films, radio broadcasts, and newspaper articles that stretched the truth about the war in order to increase support of the Nazi agenda. Because he was so good at persuading people—because he was such a good liar—historians today are not exactly sure what he felt and did at different times. Still, most agree that his actions contributed to the triumph of hate in Germany.

CHAPTER ONE

EARLY LIFE AND EDUCATION

Born on October 29, 1897, to Fritz and Katharina Goebbels, Joseph Goebbels was very sickly as a child. First he caught pneumonia and nearly died. He also suffered a terrible fever and had hallucinations. Then, when he was barely four years old, Joseph came down with a rare, painful disease that made it impossible for him to walk. Doctors eventually diagnosed it as osteomyelitis, a bone infection that can, in rare cases, cause a permanent disability.

Joseph happened to be one of those rare cases. Despite all of his parents' and doctors' efforts, his right leg remained crippled. It would always be shorter than the left. When he was ten, a last-ditch operation failed, leaving him with a clubfoot forever.

Though his full name was Paul Joseph Goebbels, Joseph and the family rarely if ever used his first name. He was born into a lower middle-class family; his father was a hardworking clerk, and his mother was a housewife. Together they had six children, including Joseph

As a teenager, Goebbels excelled in school. He went on to earn a doctorate in German philology, the study of language in written historical sources.

and an older sister who died when she was still an infant. Like his two older brothers and two younger sisters, Joseph was raised as a Catholic. His mother often brought Joseph to the local church to pray that whatever sin had led to his crippling disease would be forgiven.

Other children would make fun of Joseph because he was deformed. They called him a cripple and much worse. He was also very short and skinny and often sick. He studied hard and got good grades, though some of his teachers resented his independent ways. He graduated from primary school to the Gymnasium, roughly the same as high school in the United States. There he worked even harder, achieving top grades in Latin, geography, German, and mathematics. He also excelled in the arts and was known as a good actor.

He did so well in school that he was chosen to give the graduation speech. Afterward, the head of the school commended him for the content of his speech. But the principal didn't think the delivery was very good. "You'll never make a good speaker," said the man. Few teachers have ever been so wrong.

HIGHER EDUCATION

When Goebbels gave his school speech in 1917, Germany was in the middle of World War I. Like many other Germans, the boy was very patriotic. So was his speech. He spoke of Germany as the fatherland and the head of the country, the kaiser, as a hero. Goebbels' words called for Germany to prove it was the leader of the world. Many young German men and women felt that way at the time and were shocked when Germany lost the war the next year. To many, it seemed as if the world had been turned upside down.

In some ways it had. Chaos and hard economic times followed the end of the war. Germany lost territory and was forced to pay large reparations to the Allies who had fought against it. Different political parties vied for power in the confusion, including the newly formed National Socialist German Workers' Party. The party was known as the NSDAP (its acronym in German) and would eventually be called the Nazi Party.

Because of his club foot, Goebbels was not able to serve in the military during the war. Instead, he enrolled in the University of Bonn in 1917, where he studied German literature and philosophy. To get his final degree, he studied a playwright from Germany's romantic period, a time of great idealism and nationalism. Goebbels earned a doctorate, the highest degree possible, from Heidelberg University in 1921. He was the first in his family to receive a Ph.D. From that day on, Goebbels preferred that he be called "Herr Doktor," or "Mister Doctor," in honor of his status.

ANTI-SEMITISM AFTER WORLD WAR I

Many biographers have tried to trace the origin of Goebbels' hatred of Jews to his early life. Some believe that specific events turned him against Jews, but it is not easy to find a specific incident that made him anti-Semitic. In fact, he does not seem to have hated Jews when he was young, or at least he did not express this hatred vehemently. During his early twenties, Goebbels had a girlfriend who was half Jewish. While going to school, he studied under Jewish professors and seems to have respected them a great deal. On the other hand, some biographers point out that he was rejected by some of these professors.

At the same time, some Germans were falsely blaming the country's economic struggles during the 1920s on Jews. Goebbels suffered during these difficult times like most others. His disability also made him feel inferior and perhaps angry. It is possible that he turned these feelings into hatred for Jews.

Anti-Semitism had a long history in Germany and Europe. Even the Catholic Church was very anti-Semitic. For much of its history, the church officially blamed Jews for the death of Jesus Christ. While conditions for Jews had improved greatly during the nineteenth and early twentieth centuries, much prejudice remained, and it only increased after Germany's humiliating defeat in

In 1924, the new German currency, the Reichsmark, helped control inflation, but people were still struggling to make ends meet, as seen by this long line outside a state loan office.

World War I. The public needed someone to blame, and the Jews were once again an easy scapegoat. Germany's defeat was not the fault of the Jews, of course, but the facts did not prevent people—both ordinary citizens and politicians—from believing hateful myths that the Jews were plotting to bring down Germany.

Goebbels was among those who fell victim to this line of thinking. Although it is difficult to determine exactly why or when he began to believe in anti-Semitic prejudice, by the time he joined the Nazi Party in 1924, it tainted everything he said and did.

BLAMING THE JEWS

According to the United States Holocaust Memorial Museum, German Jews served in the army during World War I at a higher rate than non-Jewish Germans. How can it be, then, that they were blamed for losing the war?

World War I had been by far the bloodiest conflict ever fought in Europe to that point. Everyone, leaders and common people alike, were looking to cast the blame for this carnage on someone else. During the postwar peace negotiations, the victors—the United Kingdom, France, the United States, and their allies—decided that Germany and Austria were at fault for starting the war and should be punished by having to pay exorbitant damages.

Understandably, this did not go over well with the German people, who felt that all the participants shared equal responsibility for the war. Radical right-wing anti-Semites started saying that the Jews were to blame for the German loss, and there were also rumors that German Jews had betrayed their country by conspiring with Communists in the newly established Soviet Union. Some German military leaders even spread this myth, not wanting the blame to fall on their own shoulders. All of these lies about Jews being traitors who wanted to destroy Germany and take over Europe were soon commonplace, so much so that people who hadn't been anti-Semitic before began to believe that the Jews were indeed their enemy.

GOEBBELS' INFLUENCES

Anti-Semitism played an important role in Goebbels' later life. So did philosophy and his understanding of history. While a university student, Goebbels read books by Friedrich Wilhelm Nietzsche and Oswald Spengler. Nietzsche was a German philosopher who believed that the human race was searching for a higher goal. He invented the myth of the Übermensch, or "superman," to express this idea. Until man evolved into the superman, all truth was relative. The concept of the superman was perverted to justify the belief that Germans were a superior race with a great destiny. Similarly, it could also be used to justify the idea that Jews were an inferior race. And the idea that truth was relative could justify manipulating facts—or lying.

Although philosopher Friedrich Nietzsche was not an anti-Semite, many Nazis later used his ideas to defend their persecution of Jews.

Goebbels was also influenced by

Spengler. Spengler wrote *The Decline of the West*, which was published just as World War I was ending. In the book, he declared that all civilizations went through a cycle of rise and decay. He believed that the West was currently declining. Studying the book depressed Goebbels, but it also hinted that a new civilization was coming.

Goebbels' study of literature, philosophy, and religion convinced him that people needed a great hero to lead them into the future. In his early twenties, Goebbels wanted to be a writer. He worked as a journalist and wrote plays and stories. Among the things that he wrote was a novel called *Michael*. Partly based on his own life, the book is about the search for a hero. Such a hero would lead the German "folk" to greater glory. The novel wasn't published until years later. By that time, Goebbels had found a real-life hero in Adolf Hitler.

CHAPTER TWO

NAZIS IN THE 1920S

By 1924, Goebbels had joined the National Socialist German Workers' Party—the Nazis. He didn't know many of the Party leaders personally, but he believed in the Party's ideals. He was sure—and over the following years, many other Germans would come to agree—that the Nazi Party was a party for the common man that would bring Germany to greatness.

MEETING HITLER

Goebbels had been a Nazi Party member for at least a year by the time he met Adolf Hitler in 1925. Hitler had recently spent time in jail for attempting to overthrow the government, a plot known as the Beer Hall Putsch. While people in the Party idolized Hitler, most Germans either didn't know who he was or dismissed him as insignificant. The Nazi Party was tiny

Hitler and Goebbels, united by their shared vision for Germany, worked together for twenty years. At the end of World War II, Goebbels committed suicide just one day after Hitler did.

and did not have much power in German politics—at least, not yet.

Goebbels was attracted to the Party because, like him, many of its members believed in socialism, disliked Communism, and hated Jews. Above all, Nazis hated the agreements that had ended World War I and wanted Germany to be a great nation. At first, Goebbels was friends with Hitler's rivals in the Party. But soon after he met Hitler in 1925, Goebbels switched sides and became one of Hitler's strongest supporters.

Hitler recognized how smart Goebbels was and appreciated that he was an inspiring speaker who worked very hard for the Party. Goebbels was even more impressed by Hitler; he liked his ideas for the country and, more important, saw Hitler as the leader Germany needed. Within weeks, he was involved in the Party fights on Hitler's side. He idolized Hitler and did everything he could to help him win. Hitler did not share Goebbels' ideals about socialism and was more willing to compromise with businessmen than Goebbels was. However, they agreed on nearly everything else—including their hatred of Jews.

A year after they first met, Hitler rewarded Goebbels by appointing him head of the Party organization in Berlin, the capital of Germany. The local party organization was called a Gau, and Goebbels' title was the Gauleiter of Berlin. In some ways, the job was a great honor. In other ways, it was the opposite.

COMMUNISTS VERSUS NAZIS

The goal of the Communist Party of Germany, or KPD, was to have a dictatorship in Germany that was modeled on the Soviet Union. Communists believed that all land should be distributed for the common good and that the government should own all industry. In its 1932 platform, the KPD appealed to the German people: "The cause of your misery is the fact that French, British, and American capitalists are exploiting German workers to get rich themselves. Germans, unite to get rid of this terrible burden."

Like the KPD, the Nazis opposed foreign influences; however, they viewed the Communists as one of the foreign threats that had to be eradicated. Other demands in the Nazi Party's 1932 platform included repealing the Treaty of Versailles between Germany and the victors of World War I, preventing further immigration of non-Germans, and disqualifying Jews from being German citizens. After Hitler became chancellor in 1933, he banned the KPD, effectively ending the power struggle between the Nazis and the Communists.

RISE OF THE NAZIS

The Nazi Party in the early and mid-1920s was unimportant. They were overshadowed by other parties, including the German Communist Party, known as the KPD. When Goebbels arrived in Berlin to take charge, no one outside of the small band of Nazis noticed. Inside the Party, different factions were vying for power.

Goebbels had to organize and expand the Party, making sure it appealed to working class people and the lower middle class. He used a variety of methods to increase its popularity: giving speeches, holding marches and rallies, and writing articles that criticized the government and attacked Jews. He also instigated riots between Nazi Party members and the Communist Party. Because the Communists were much stronger than the Nazis, Goebbels was able to make his people look like victims in these

On May 1, 1923, the SA trained at Oberwisenfeld Army Airfield in Munich in preparation for an attack against the Communists.

fights, which helped the Party gain sympathy as well as attention.

The Nazi Party organization had a group of men called the Sturmabteilung, or storm troopers. The name is often abbreviated to SA. SA members dressed in brown uniforms when they marched and provided security for Party events. They were often used to do the Party's dirty work, like harassing other speakers or attacking enemies. Violence became an important tool in Goebbels' plans. Often a rally would start with a speech and end with the SA fighting Communists or others. He made the SA members into heroes and martyrs.

In his speeches and newspaper writings, Goebbels called for Germany to awaken and overthrow the current government. He denounced Communism as "Jewish Marxism," and Jews were considered the ultimate enemy. He called them parasites, demons, destroyers, and much worse. Like other Nazis, he focused many of his verbal attacks on Jewish people, sometimes focusing on individuals, but more often criticizing them en masse as an inferior race. Goebbels' work soon paid off as the Nazi Party became very powerful in Berlin. People across Germany began

to take notice of the Nazis—and the man some called the clubfooted demon.

Success led to opposition. Other political parties attacked the Nazis, as did the police and

In the 1920s and early 1930s, police often tried to prevent SA violence by stopping SA members and searching them for weapons.

government. They cracked down with laws and arrests. Goebbels and other Nazi leaders found ingenious ways around these measures. When the SA was banned from meeting, for example, Goebbels turned the units into bowling clubs, which naturally were allowed to meet. And Goebbels used confrontations with the authorities to boost the Nazi image. Arrests and trials kept Nazis in the news, and they won more adherents and members as their ideas became better known. Their speeches, especially those against Jews, helped them gain support.

Still, the Party did poorly in elections. In 1928, the Nazis received only 2.6 percent of the national vote for membership in the Reichstag, the German parliament. Of the approximately five hundred seats in the Reichstag, the Nazis had only twelve. One of them, however, belonged to Joseph Goebbels.

CHAPTER THREE

NAZI POWER AND PROPAGANDA

Though a member of the Reichstag, Goebbels believed the government should be overthrown. He and other Nazis were using the Reichstag only to gain power. They hoped to establish a dictatorship, with Hitler in power, which they believed was the only way to force permanent change.

Still, being a member of the Reichstag had its advantages. For one thing, Goebbels could not be arrested. This meant that he could not be charged with slandering people in his speeches, which had been a major problem before he was elected. As one of the most vocal and radical members of the Nazi Party, Goebbels was occasionally in conflict with other Nazis, even Hitler. This was not because Hitler did not share most of his beliefs but because Goebbels sometimes stirred up too much trouble.

Goebbels was closer to the country's working poor than many Nazi leaders, including Hitler. He had little use for most of the rich, whom he called the bourgeoisie. But none of these conflicts stopped Goebbels' rise in the Party. He was

Gauleiter of Berlin and the Party's propagandist, in charge of spreading information about the Nazis and helping to run their campaigns.

NAZI POPULARITY GROWS

Besides his own speeches, Goebbels used radio, posters, handouts, and even records to get the Nazi message to voters. He helped create the image of Hitler as father and Führer, or leader, of Germany. He knew that if he could do this, people would respond to Hitler with emotion rather than intellect, which would help the Nazis.

As always, Goebbels used violence to attract attention to the Party and to punish people like Communists or Jews whom he felt were the enemy. Communists fought open battles with Nazis. In fact, Communists often instigated many of the fights. When Jews protested to the police about the persecution they faced from Nazis, the perpetrators were often arrested for their crimes. Still, by making Jews scapegoats, the Nazis gained in popularity. Many Germans did not hate Jews, and some even tried to help them. But not enough Germans cared to prevent the Nazis from persecuting them. In this instance, hate was a stronger emotion than brotherhood or kindness.

Besides Goebbels' methods, several other factors helped the Nazis increase in popularity during the late 1920s and early 1930s. Hitler himself was

This 1930 propaganda poster promotes Hitler as "our final hope."

a charismatic leader, and people were attracted by his forceful personality as well as his promises to return Germany to greatness. Many Germans feared a Communist takeover because the German Communist party had strong links to the Soviet Union,

GOEBBELS' MARRIAGE

As hard as he worked, Goebbels found time for love. In 1930, he met a well-to-do divorcée named Magda Quandt. She had recently joined the Party even though her stepfather was a Jew. Magda was a beautiful woman in her late twenties who appeared elegant and self-assured. One of Goebbels' biographers, Ralf Georg Reuth, says she saw Goebbels as an idealist and a fighter. She may also have been attracted to his growing power.

Goebbels was attracted to her beauty. It is possible that because of his disability, he was flattered by the attention of such an elegant and accomplished woman. Magda also encouraged and supported his ideals. At first their love affair stumbled—she was seeing another man. But soon Goebbels won her heart, charming her with attention and gifts. They were married in a civil ceremony in December 1931, with Adolf Hitler as one of the witnesses.

which many Germans considered the enemy. People also became disillusioned with the other political parties, which made promises they couldn't fulfill.

But most important were the troubled times. At the end of the 1920s, Germany and the rest of the world entered a severe depression. Many Germans were out of work and, worse, lost their life savings when banks failed. The government was even more strapped for cash because of World War I reparations. Foreign troops occupied German land to enforce these claims, reminding people how weak the present German government was.

THE JULY 1932 ELECTIONS

In spring 1932, Goebbels had helped convince Hitler to run for president of Germany. Even though Hitler had lost, the election had greatly increased Nazi prestige. The Nazis were gaining momentum heading into the Reichstag election that July. On July 9, Goebbels gave a powerful speech at a vast stadium in Berlin known as the Lustgarten.

"I represent the greatest movement ever seen on German soil," Goebbels began. From that moment, two hundred thousand ears listened to every word, every nuance he uttered. Though short and skinny, Goebbels had a voice that could thunder during a speech. He dressed simply, with a plain suit and faded overcoat. His figure seemed to grow as he spoke. His narrow face and hands darted about as

Thanks in part to Goebbels' persuasive campaigning, the Nazi Party became the biggest party in the Reichstag in 1932.

he talked of Germany as "the fatherland." As always, he had carefully planned this speech beforehand. Goebbels often practiced his technique in front of a mirror and made dramatic gestures to emphasize his points.

This day he spoke of Nazism as a religion. He inspired men to hate the fatherland's enemies—Communists and Jews. "Fate has given us a chance," he said. His frenzied voice stoked the crowd. "The day of freedom and prosperity is coming!"

Goebbels sometimes used planted audience members and even recorded applause to help amplify his talents as a speaker. But he didn't need these things. Many people who watched his speeches believed he was second only to Hitler as a speaker; some even thought he was better.

His words often contrasted the chaos of the present with an ideal picture of Germany's former greatness. Goebbels' speeches claimed that the Nazis were struggling against powerful enemies: the Communists, Jews, and the bourgeoisie. His other rhetorical tactics included quoting poetry and comparing the Nazis to mythic and legendary beings. Again and again he repeated the Nazi slogan: "Germany Awake!"

In Goebbels' mind, the German people had to rise up against their enemies. They had to reclaim the greatness of Germany and restore the economy. The path to achieving this required removing the Communists and Jews and bringing Adolf Hitler—"our Führer"—to power. "Idealism lives in Germany," Goebbels shouted as the crowd went wild. "The people can be shown the way!"

Goebbels' hard work in the July Reichstag campaign paid off. The Nazis won more seats than ever before, going from an insignificant party to an incredibly important force in German politics. Although they did not control an absolute majority, they held more seats than any other party. It was the latest and greatest in a series of remarkable victories.

NAZI STRENGTH

The German system of government, a parliamentary system, was very different than that of the United States. Ordinarily, the leader of the majority party in the Reichstag was chosen by the president to be the chancellor and run the government. When no party had an absolute majority, the parties would have to work together by forming a coalition government. One party's leader would fill the chancellor's post, but he would have to work with members of other parties, who would be appointed as ministers. For example, one minister might be in charge of the army, while another might be in charge of dealing with foreign countries. Many parliamentary governments continue to work this way today.

Twice in 1932, the Nazis were offered the chance to join coalition governments. But Hitler rejected the offers, since he would not be appointed chancellor. He thought these offers would weaken his power. Since the Nazis were getting stronger, he believed he could wait. Either the Nazis would eventually win an absolute majority, or they would be offered the chancellor post. Either way, he would win. The refusal of the Nazis to participate in the coalitions made the government weak. It also kept the Nazis from being linked or associated with these governments when they failed.

Historians have debated how strong the Nazi Party actually was. Many look at the elections held in 1932 and 1933 and see that the Nazis did less well in some areas than others and failed to gain an absolute majority. These historians believe the Party had reached its peak and Germans were already rejecting the Nazi agenda.

It is true that the Party lost some support among middle-class voters in the late 1932 and early 1933 elections. It is not clear, however, why. It may have been because of a change in party strategy. Goebbels is sometimes blamed for policies that were aimed at the working class and were not popular with the middle class. The reasons may also have been a lack of funds and energy, or voters rejecting the Nazi agenda.

In any event, during 1932 and 1933 the Nazis were a powerful force in Germany. In all of the elections, a large portion of the population voted for them. Their agenda was well known, thanks to Goebbels. At the beginning of 1933, they held the biggest bloc in the Reichstag and showed no sign of disappearing in a few months.

The Nazi power went far beyond the Reichstag. Many policemen and soldiers were Party members as well, leading to many rumors that they would rebel and help Hitler form a new government. Rumors also swirled about a takeover by the Communists, though they did not have many supporters in the police or army.

These rumors put much pressure on the coalition governments and police. Demonstrations by Nazis and Communists, labor strikes, and the continuing economic hardships put even more pressure on the government. Germany was engulfed in political chaos.

HINDENBURG AND HITLER

In January 1933, Hitler was asked to join a coalition government for the third time. But this time, President Paul von Hindenburg offered Hitler the post of chancellor. This was what Hitler had been waiting for. Even though many positions in the cabinet would be held by the Nazis' enemies, Hitler gladly accepted. He and the other Nazi leaders were confident they could dominate the government that way. It was a great victory. "It is almost a dream," Goebbels wrote in his diary. "A fairy tale . . . The revolution has begun."

Historians are not sure why Hindenburg offered Hitler the chancellorship. He may have feared a rebellion in the army and police that would give Hitler total power. He may have been afraid the Communists would take over. He may also have thought Hitler would soften his political agenda and accept compromise.

There is also the possibility that the Nazis blackmailed him. Hitler had found out that Hindenburg had benefited greatly from a law passed several years before. A well-respected war hero, Hindenburg had managed to pass his property to his son without a substantial estate tax. It is possible that Hindenburg and his son, who was an important advisor to him, were worried about the scandal. Another factor may have been Hindenburg's age. He was tired of all the intrigue and chaos, and some believed that he was becoming senile.

While many people were skeptical, some leaders thought Hitler and the Nazis could be controlled and would fully abide by the law. They were sadly mistaken. As soon as he gained power, Hitler began

The ministers of Hitler's 1933 cabinet, including Goebbels, Hermann Göring, and Heinrich Himmler, continued to be close advisers throughout World War II.

moving Party leaders into important positions. Among them was Goebbels, who was appointed minister for propaganda and culture. At thirty-five, he was the youngest member of the cabinet. His job was to help determine the regulations governing all media and art in the country. Eventually, he would control all of the media and shape the public's image of the Nazi Party and Hitler.

Goebbels also planned to use propaganda as a "sword" against Jews and Communists. He hoped to stir up the German people so they would see the Nazi policies as the nation's best path toward economic stability and strength. One of the ways he would do this was by controlling the information people received and by manipulating facts to his advantage.

MINISTER FOR PROPAGANDA AND CULTURE

Goebbels used a number of strategies to further the Nazi cause. Though he was not above violence, some of his methods were the same as those used by modern election and advertising campaigns. He emphasized the strong points of his argument and downplayed or did not mention the bad points of Hitler and the Nazi Party.

Goebbels also distorted the truth and lied. He used his power to shut down or intimidate newspapers that opposed Nazis, especially the Jewish press. He could have a reporter he didn't like fired. He made sure that films, articles, and radio shows favoring the Nazis appeared, as well as anti-Semitic material.

Goebbels sometimes disdained the German public as sheep who could be manipulated easily. However, some of his methods of persuasion would not have worked if people had not been willing to hear out his message. Modern advertising works the same way.

Many Germans wanted to be persuaded that Hitler would solve their problems, that he was the great leader who could save the country. Some Germans also hated Jews. Goebbels was able to take advantage of these things during the elections. He used logical arguments to convince people that the

Preis 30 Pfennig

Ritualmord-Nummer

Der Stürmer

[De]utsches Wochenblatt zum Kampfe um die Wahrheit

HERAUSGEBER: JULIUS STREICHER

Sonder-Nummer 1		Nürnberg, im Mai 1934		12. Jahr 1934

Jüdischer Mordplan

gegen die nichtjüdische Menschheit aufgedeckt

Das Mördervolk

Die Juden leben in der ganzen Welt in einem furchtbaren Verdacht. Wer ihn nicht kennt, der kennt die Judenfrage nicht. Wer die Juden nur ansieht, wie Heinrich Heine (Chaim Bückeburg) sie beschreibt: „Ein Volk, das zu seinem Unterhalt mit Wechseln und alten Hosen handelt und [illegible] Uniform die [illegible] auf falschem Wege. Wer aber weiß, welch eine ungeheuerliche Anklage schon seit Anbeginn gegen die Juden erhoben wird, dem erscheint dieses Volk in einem anderen Lichte. Er sieht in ihnen nicht nur ein eigenartiges, seltsam anmutendes Volk, er sieht in ihnen Verbrecher und Mörder und Teufel in Menschengestalt. Und es überkommt ihn gegen dieses Volk ein heiliger Zorn und Haß.

Der Verdacht, in dem die Juden stehen, ist der des Menschenmordes. Sie werden bezichtigt, nichtjüdische Kinder und nichtjüdische Erwachsene an sich zu locken, sie zu schlachten und ihnen das Blut abzuzapfen. Sie werden bezichtigt, dieses Blut in die Mazzen (ungesäuertes Brot) zu verbacken und auch sonstige abergläubische Zauberei damit zu treiben. Sie werden bezichtigt, ihre Opfer, besonders die Kinder, dabei furchtbar zu martern und zu foltern. Und während dieses Folterns Drohungen, Flüche und Verwünschungen gegen die Nichtjuden auszustoßen. Dieser planmäßig betriebene Menschenmord hat eine besondere Bezeichnung, er heißt

Ritualmord.

Das Wissen vom jüdischen Ritualmord ist schon Jahrtausende alt. Es ist so alt wie die Juden selbst. Die Nichtjuden haben es von Generation zu Generation übertragen. Es ist uns durch Schriften überliefert. Es ist aber auch in der breiten Volksmasse vorhanden. In den verstecktesten Bauerndörfern stößt man auf dieses Wissen. Der Ahne sprach von ihm zu seinem Enkel. Und dieser wieder trug es weiter auf Kinder und Kindeskinder. So vererbte es sich bis zum heutigen Tag.

Es ist auch in den anderen Völkern vorhanden. Wo irgendwo in der Welt eine Leiche gefunden wird, die die Anzeichen des Ritualmordes trägt, erhebt sich sofort laut und groß die Anklage. Sie richtet sich überall nur gegen die Juden. Hunderte und aberhunderte von Völkern, Stämmen und Rassen bewohnen den Erdball. Niemand denkt daran, sie des planmäßigen Kindermordes zu beschuldigen und sie als Mördervolk zu bezeichnen. Den Juden allein wird diese Anklage aus allen Völkern entgegengeschleudert. Und viele große Männer haben

Judenopfer

Durch die Jahrtausende vergoß der Jud, geheimem Ritus folgend, Menschenblut
Der Teufel sitzt uns heute noch im Nacken, es liegt an Euch die Teufelsbrut zu packen

Die Juden sind unser Unglück!

Der Stürmer, an anti-Semitic newspaper, promoted a "Jewish murder plan" and declared "the Jews are our misfortune" in a May 1934 edition.

Nazis were the answer to the country's problems—and that the Jews were to blame for them. He also staged mass demonstrations to stir up patriotism and make Germans feel good—not just about Hitler, but about themselves. Once he was made propaganda minister, he had even more power to boost the Nazi agenda.

Not every Nazi liked Goebbels. Some referred to him as "Satan" and worse, believing he was so power hungry that he would do anything to get ahead. At the same time, many were jealous of his position in the Party.

THE REICHSTAG FIRE

On February 27, 1933, shortly after Hitler became chancellor and right before a new election to the Reichstag was held, the Reichstag building burned. At the time, Communist Party members were talking about open revolt against the new Nazi-dominated government. The Nazis immediately charged that the fire was part of a Communist plot against the government and country.

Most historians believe the fire was started by a Communist Party member. Some, however, think the

fire was part of a Nazi plot to take over. If so, Goebbels would probably have been part of it. He had planned a major rally for a few days after the fire. He

The Reichstag fire left behind only a burnt shell of the building's dome.

had used different means against the Communists before and was certainly not opposed to employing violence or arson to get what he wanted.

On the other hand, Hitler, Goebbels, and other Nazi leaders like Hermann Göring seemed to be taken by surprise by the fire. If it was just an act, it was a very good one. And despite years during which they could have done so, the Nazis never promoted a theory of a real conspiracy to burn down the Reichstag. They might have arranged evidence of one if they had been behind the plot. And besides, Hitler had already been concentrating power in his own hands before the fire.

Whatever the truth, Hitler did use the disaster to ask for "emergency" powers that made him a dictator. The fire convinced many people—not just Nazis—that these powers were justified. Goebbels helped justify the power grab, making sure that people heard about the Communists' plans. Once Hitler had "emergency" control, he never gave it up.

CHAPTER FOUR

KRISTALLNACHT AND INCREASED ANTI-SEMITISM

As they gradually took control of the country, the Nazis' hatred of Jews turned into official government policy. They started with a boycott of Jewish businesses on April 1, 1933. Goebbels helped organize and publicize this boycott to put pressure on Jews. SA men stood in Jewish stores and tried to bully people to leave.

The boycott was not as successful as Goebbels and others wanted. Jews remained in Germany, although they were fearful. The Nazis did not let up. As propaganda minister, Goebbels tried to remove Jews from all important jobs in the media and arts. In 1935, he helped establish a series of anti-Jewish laws known as the Nuremberg Laws that severely limited Jewish life in Germany. The longer he was in office, the more his hatred of Jews seems to have grown.

At times, however, Goebbels could make it seem as if he wasn't radically anti-Semitic. In fact, on Yom Kippur in 1935, Goebbels gave a speech denouncing anti-Semitic violence. The Nuremberg Laws were advertised, under his guidance, as laws that would protect Jews.

Furthermore, Goebbels helped "clean up" the image of the Nazi Party before the 1936 Olympics, toning down attacks against Jews. But that was just an act during the Olympics, which was an opportunity for the Nazis to showcase their strength to their enemies around the world. Hitler wanted other nations to admire Germany's athletic prowess and ability to put on a fantastic large-scale event; he did not want them to associate Germany with prejudice.

Nonetheless, Goebbels wanted to rid Germany of Jews. It is difficult to say if, at this point in his life, he was in favor of mass murder of Jews. He left no evidence that he was. But he knew that his speeches and urgings would incite others to hurt and kill Jews, which would help accomplish his ultimate goal—removal of all Jews from Germany. If he had any moral reservations about these deaths, he never expressed them. He believed his goal of racial purity justified any means.

THE NIGHT OF BROKEN GLASS

On November 9, 1938, Nazi Party members gathered in the Old City Hall in Munich. The party had been in power for more than five years, but each year it celebrated the anniversary of the Beer Hall Putsch, Hitler's failed rebellion in 1923.

Suddenly, a murmur began going through the crowd. A German diplomat had been shot in France. Hitler and Goebbels quickly conferred, and Hitler left. Goebbels made his way to the podium. His voice was sober, but his words were frantic as he told the party members that a Polish Jew had killed a German diplomat, Ernst von Rath, in Paris. Germans were outraged. Already, they were rioting against "international Jewry" in the streets. These riots, Goebbels carefully noted, had not been started by the Party or the government. But the government would not prevent them either. The calmness left his voice. His speech became a rant against Jews, as hateful as any he had ever given.

Outside in the streets of Munich, Goebbels' hatred was underlined by rocks thrown through windows, gasoline ignited on buildings, punches smashed into innocent faces. There were riots, assaults, and murders all across Germany. So many windows were broken that the destruction would soon be known as Kristallnacht, or the Night of Broken Glass.

Many of the thugs carrying out the violence were members of the SA and SS, Nazi Party organizations. Contrary to what Goebbels claimed, the government had indeed been involved. The police

After Kristallnacht, pedestrians snicker at the broken windows of a Jewish-owned shop in Berlin.

stood by and watched during the riots. And before the action was over, more than thirty thousand Jews would be imprisoned in concentration camps, large prisons used by Nazis to punish their enemies. Although most of the Kristallnacht Jews would soon be released, their detainment was an ominous sign of things to come.

GOEBBELS' AFFAIRS

The evidence is not clear, but many historians believe that Goebbels played an important role in arranging for Kristallnacht. If so, he would have had other motives besides sheer hatred. Since becoming propaganda minister, Goebbels' life had changed dramatically. Although he was an important member of the Nazi Party, Goebbels was poor. For many years he borrowed money from his parents. Even when he was elected to the Reichstag, his finances were limited. It was whispered within the Party that he took money from the treasury to meet personal debts.

Everything changed when the Nazis gained power. Goebbels received a generous salary and a large "official" home as propaganda minister. Hitler later arranged for a publisher to buy the rights to Goebbels' diary. That meant that Goebbels would receive a large amount of money for the diary, which would be published and sold in the future. Since Goebbels was already writing the diary, this was a large windfall. It enabled him and his wife to buy an estate near Berlin. (It also helped future historians, since it helped guarantee that he would continue writing the diary.) But all of this success may have complicated Goebbels' life.

During the 1920s, Goebbels had risen to become one of the most important people in the Nazi Party. Now that the Nazis ran the government, he was one of the most important people in all of Germany. Films and theater were under his control. He began to meet young actors and actresses and have affairs with some of the actresses.

One of these affairs was very serious. During the 1936 Olympics, Goebbels met an actress named Lida Baarová. They quickly fell in love. In the meantime, Goebbels' relationship with his wife Magda had soured. They raised six children together, as well as a son by Magda's first marriage. But their relationship grew stormier as Goebbels' power grew—and as the affair with Baarová grew more and more serious.

Hitler clearly disapproved and may have taken Magda's side in the dispute. One of Goebbels' biographer, Ralf Georg Reuth, points out that this sex scandal damaged Goebbels' position in the Party. It also threatened his friendship with Hitler, which was an important source of power. It was also much more. Goebbels worshiped the Führer as a god and would do anything to win Hitler's approval. Threatened with losing favor, he may have searched for a way to get back on Hitler's good side. Persecuting Jews was a sure way to do this. Reuth suggests that Kristallnacht might have been planned by Goebbels partly because of his problems.

Goebbels was also involved in a power struggle with the SS and its leader, Heinrich Himmler. In a way, the riots threatened Himmler, showing that Goebbels could call on many thugs if he needed support.

RESTRICTIONS ON JEWS

Whether he planned all of Kristallnacht or just inspired it, whether he was motivated by politics or sheer hate, Goebbels approved of the riots against Jews. Immediately after Kristallnacht, Goebbels was appointed to a commission headed by Hermann

Demonstrating the reach of anti-Semitism beyond Germany, this sign announces that Jews are undesirable in the Austrian town of Gleisdorf.

Göring. Himmler was another member of the group. These men, the most important in the government after Hitler, were supposed to figure out what to do with Jews. In their words, they were supposed to solve the "Jewish question."

The commission did not "solve" anything. It did, however, increase discrimination against Jews. Goebbels backed new laws banning Jews from many jobs and requiring segregation measures, such as separate railroad cars for Jews and other Germans. Payments from insurance companies for damage done on Kristallnacht would go to the government, not the Jews. Worse, Jews would have to pay the government a fine of one billion Reichmarks as "punishment" for murdering the German diplomat.

SEVENTY-FIVE YEARS LATER

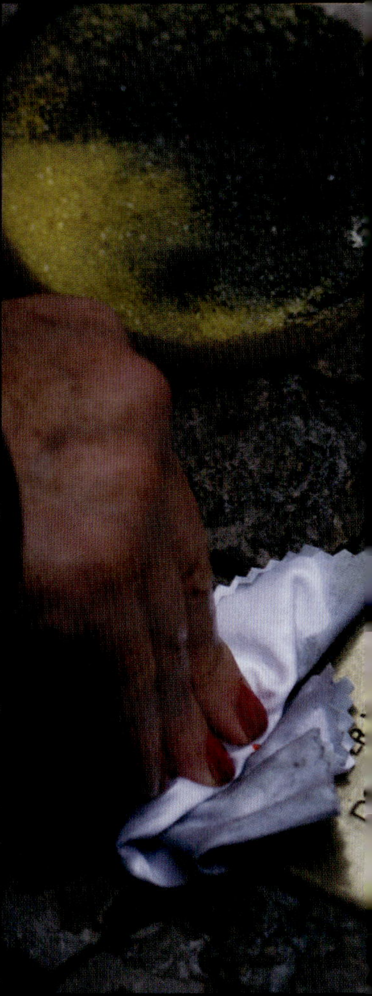

Each year on the anniversary of Kristallnacht, Germany remembers the victims with speeches and museum exhibitions. The seventy-fifth anniversary in 2013 included additional commemorations focused on explaining Kristallnacht's significance to young people and others who were unaware of how it contributed to the government's systematic persecution against Jews. In Berlin, dozens of shops made it look like their windows had been broken, just as they were in November 1938. *Stolpersteine*, or stumbling blocks, bearing the names of victims have been placed in the sidewalks outside their homes, and the government led an effort to polish and clean the stones for the seventy-fifth anniversary. In her remarks, German chancellor Angela Merkel called Kristallnacht "one of the darkest moments in German history" and reminded people that "we must always remember our past so we can look responsibly into the future."

These stones honor victims of the pogrom on the night of November 9–10, 1938.

JEWISH EMIGRATION

The Kristallnacht riots were deplored around the world. It was clear that the actions had been sanctioned by the government. Until this time, many Jews were unsure how far Hitler and Goebbels would go. While Goebbels' speeches made it clear that he hated Jews, most Jews had dealt with this type of prejudice before. It seemed likely that the government would harass Jews and limit their freedom, but go no further.

Jews in Germany had seen conditions greatly improve during the nineteenth and twentieth centuries. Many felt more German than Jewish. They had fought in the German army during World War I and did not believe their country would ever reject them. Many may have felt that the Nazis were a temporary problem. They didn't like the prejudice, but they were willing to wait it out because they weren't powerful enough to stop it and didn't want to leave the country.

But Kristallnacht convinced many Jews that the Nazis would stop at nothing, not even murder. There was a massive increase in emigration. Prior to 1933, there were 500,000 to 525,000 Jews in Germany. By the start of 1938, about a quarter of them had left the country. In the ten months after Kristallnacht, somewhere between 100,000 and 150,000 emigrated.

A large portion of those who remained behind were in their forties and older. Some stayed because they felt they were too old to start life over in another country. Some didn't have the money to leave, since the Nazis charged exorbitant fees before granting permission. Others weren't able to find

Jewish children who fled anti-Semitism in Germany arrive in London in February 1939.

countries to take them. Many countries, including the United States, had immigration quotas and strict visa requirements that prevented most Jewish refugees from leaving Germany.

Less than a week after Kristallnacht, President Roosevelt condemned it in a press conference, stating, "The news of the past few days from Germany has deeply shocked public opinion in the United States ... I myself could scarcely believe that such things could occur in a twentieth-century civilization." A few months before Kristallnacht, he had called a conference in Evian, France, to address the refugee crisis, but it did not help. Though the Dominican Republic agreed to welcome more refugees, the other thirty-one nations that attended refused to alter their existing immigration restraints to help German Jews.

GENTILE REACTION

After Kristallnacht, few Jews had any illusions about the Nazis. The attitude of non-Jews, or Gentiles, was more complicated. By this time, the Nazis had firm control of the police, meaning anyone who openly opposed Hitler could be arrested, tortured, and killed. So it is not surprising that there was not much public criticism of the government or Kristallnacht.

Still, there were many courageous Germans who defied the Nazis by helping Jews. Some were even Party members or policemen. This help ranged from merely shopping at a Jewish-owned store to not volunteering information to hiding a Jew wanted by the authorities. In a few instances, Germans stopped thugs from hurting Jews on Kristallnacht. It would be a mistake to think that all Germans approved of the Nazi actions against the Jews.

At the same time, many people also sincerely believed that Hitler was doing a good job as leader. There were pictures of him in many homes. In addition to its adult party membership, the Nazis drew in children and teenagers who joined the Hitler Youth. Some of these people felt Kristallnacht was justified. Some hated Jews to begin with, blaming them for the country's troubles. Others were not so sure but supported Hitler anyway.

Goebbels' most important job during this period was to bolster Hitler's image. He filled the airwaves with positive reports that touted the improved German economy, treated Hitler as a god, and denounced Jews as the enemy.

CHAPTER FIVE

THE FINAL SOLUTION

Two months after the German army invaded Poland, causing Britain and France to declare war on Germany and initiate World War II, Goebbels visited Lodz, Poland.

The Polish army had been annihilated almost immediately. Goebbels had never had a high opinion of Poland, but the squalor he saw on November 2, 1939, boggled his mind— the Jewish ghetto worst of all. It didn't seem fit for animals. Goebbels thought the Jews were swine, wallowing in their mud and squalor.

Hans Frank, the governor of the conquered lands, led Goebbels on the tour. Frank talked about the problems of governing the conquered land. Even though sixty thousand ethnic Germans had lived here before the war, Frank feared rebellion. And there were a variety of other problems dealing with these "backward" people. This would not be an easy place to nourish the new ideal of German culture.

Goebbels had to agree that it would be difficult. But the first step seemed obvious to him—eliminate the Jews. Though Frank did not

Joseph Goebbels is welcomed with Nazi salutes as he arrives at a rally in Gdinya, Poland.

disagree, the German army, or Wehrmacht, was making this hard. The Wehrmacht, as Goebbels told his diary later, chose to pursue a "bourgeois" policy—not a "racial" one. Therefore, he determined to prevent the army from interfering.

"[The Jews] are animals," Goebbels wrote in his diary. "Our task is no longer humanitarian but surgical. Steps must be taken, and they must be radical ones, make no mistake." Immediately after his return from Poland, Goebbels went to see Hitler. He urged that Jews be removed from Germany. What else he may have urged at that meeting is not precisely clear.

Some Jews were being taken to concentration camps, but Goebbels wanted the removal of every single Jew from Germany. Despite his continued urgings, mass deportations did not begin until 1941, after the invasion of Russia.

THE FINAL SOLUTION

Hitler had always believed that the German nation should dominate Europe. Like Goebbels, he believed the Germans were a master race that needed to evict lesser races from their territory so that they would have "living space." Hitler viewed parts of Austria, Czechoslovakia, and Poland as natural German territory because historically, Germans had either lived in these areas or had much influence there. He also wanted to dominate France and occupy Russia.

An important part of Hitler's plans included the elimination of Jews from Europe. When the war began, he made it clear to those around him that the Jews should be eliminated. The plan to do so became known as the Final Solution. In the end, millions of Jews and other "inferior races" would be killed by the Nazis.

There is much debate over exactly how the plans for the Final Solution evolved. We know what the end result was: millions of people were murdered in factories of death. But it is difficult to know all of the particulars about the decision to implement Hitler's wishes. It is not clear, for example, when he made the decision to slaughter Jews. Historians still debate whether he planned to do so before taking power or whether he gradually reached this decision.

Hitler intended this slaughter, though he notably never wrote down an order to kill millions of Jews. His top lieutenants, like Goebbels, did not either. But the records of other officials below them reveal the extent of their planning. And the evidence of their actions is plentiful: documents to the concentration camps themselves, as well as the testimony of Nazis during the Nuremberg Trials after the war.

Most historians now believe that the Nazi plans for the Final Solution went through several stages. Before the war, Nazi leaders may have hoped simply to get Jews to leave Germany and Europe. In the early stages of the war, some Nazi officials favored making Madagascar, an island off Africa, a Jewish colony. Collecting Jews in ghettos and concentration camps would have helped plans to ship them there. Records of Goebbels' staff meetings in 1940 include references to this plan. If this was the plan, it changed during the early years of World War II. It may have changed for practical reasons; shipping Jews out of the country would have been difficult. Or it may have changed because the Nazis preferred complete elimination of their enemies.

Hitler, Goebbels, and the others always wanted to remove Jews from Germany and Europe. Their policies were always anti-Semitic, and they clearly did not consider the murder of a Jew a serious crime. By the summer of 1941, the SS was exterminating Jews in a massive, well-planned operation.

GOEBBELS' ROLE IN THE HOLOCAUST

Goebbels was not a camp guard or prison official and did not personally command the men who put others to death. His responsibilities were primarily in Germany, not in conquered territory, which is where most Jews were killed. He was not the Führer, whose wish for the elimination of the Jews was known and understood by all of his subordinates.

However, Goebbels still bears responsibility for the millions killed. Various biographers and historians have arrived at slightly different conclusions about Goebbels' role in the Holocaust. Some believe he was not very important. They compare him to people like Himmler, who commanded those who murdered millions. Others believe he played an important and direct role.

Each view depends on a slightly different interpretation of facts. For example, biographer Ralf Georg Reuth argues that Goebbels tried to convince Hitler to exterminate Jews after he visited Lodz in 1939. In Reuth's opinion, this helped lead the Nazis to the plans for the Holocaust. It can be argued, however, that Goebbels' urgings had less influence than those of people who wanted to force Jews to emigrate. It can also be argued that Goebbels himself may have favored the emigration plan, at least for a time.

Still, Goebbels' actions show that he was deeply involved in the Final Solution. He whipped up the public's hatred of Jews from the start of his career and worked with Göring on the committee formed to deal with the "Jewish question" after Kristallnacht. He made it impossible for Jews to hold jobs in the arts or cultural organizations and incited and organized violence against them. As Gauleiter of Berlin, he did everything he could to have Jews removed from the city. He continually urged Hitler to take action against the Jews.

Goebbels also knew of the concentration camps and the plans for extermination. By controlling the media, he suppressed news of the extermination, which he judged would harm the Nazi image.

CONVINCING THE PUBLIC TO SUPPORT THE WAR

Goebbels was nervous about World War II when it began in 1939. He knew that Germany would struggle if it had to fight on two fronts at the same time. Like many others, he was worried that Great Britain and France would attack from the west while German troops were in Poland. Similarly, he was wary about invading the Soviet Union in the east.

Even so, he was in favor of Hitler's war aims. In 1940, with France conquered and England quivering, Goebbels envisioned a united Europe—a German Europe. He believed that advances in transportation and media made it necessary to bring more unity and order to the continent. Of course, he also believed that this effort should be dominated by Nazis. Like the philosophers he had studied in college, Goebbels believed that a new age was dawning in which the Nazis were the "supermen" who would form a new civilization.

Even before the conflict began, Goebbels helped lay the groundwork for public acceptance of World War II. He had stories published and broadcast that accused each country in turn of provoking the Germans. As the war continued, he tried to make sure the public supported it by ordering stories emphasizing German victories. Of course, his job "selling" the war was helped by the easy victories that the German army won in

FORBIDDEN FILMS

Under Goebbels during World War II, the Nazi Ministry of Propaganda produced over twelve hundred films. Around forty of these are considered so offensive that the German government continues to ban public screenings of them, unless accompanied by an educational discussion to provide context; they also may be found on the Internet. In a 2015 documentary, *Forbidden Films*, filmmaker Felix Moeller explores whether this ban is effective or right. After all, it is reminiscent of the Nazis' own censorship of opposing viewpoints, and it can be argued that banning the films only increases interest in them.

However, others are afraid that this old propaganda could still be effective and also lead to more anti-Semitism. This is especially dangerous because anti-Semitism has been on the rise in certain sectors of Europe in recent years. Moeller's documentary demonstrates that there is still no easy answer about what to do with Goebbels' propaganda, even many decades later.

the war's early years. But he also emphasized the sacrifices and hard work of German soldiers and common people during the war.

The Allies called Goebbels "the big liar" during the war. But a careful review of German news bulletins about the war, especially during the early years, shows that most were not false at all. While they certainly favored Germany, they did not make outrageous claims that could not be backed up with facts. Some historians say that reports issued under Goebbels' control were generally more truthful than Allied reports.

Goebbels believed that it was best for a propagandist not to lie. On the contrary, since he wanted people to believe what they heard, he took pains to present accurate pictures. But he often left out details that would hurt his position or that he knew his audience wouldn't like. For example, instead of

The Ministry of Propaganda controlled most of the German press during World War II.

reporting about Nazi crimes, he would spread information about Allied crimes. In this way, he could use the truth as a weapon. And anyone hearing Allied claims about German acts would remember the claims about what the Allies did.

OPERATION BARBAROSSA

By the spring of 1941, Hitler had decided it was time to fight the war on two fronts, and he initiated Operation Barbarossa, the plan to invade the Soviet Union. He told Goebbels to launch a massive misinformation campaign. Goebbels' job was to make sure that rumors were spread that Great Britain, not the Soviet Union, was about to be invaded. Part of his campaign included making believe that he had fallen out of favor with Hitler, which he had not.

This misinformation campaign didn't fool the British, who warned the USSR of Hitler's plans. Soviet spies also warned their leaders that an attack was coming. But the Soviet Union was still caught by surprise by the first German tanks.

Immediately after the invasion, Goebbels once again pushed for the immediate removal of the remaining Jews from Berlin and all of Germany. He wanted them immediately deported to Poland. He may have wanted them to be exterminated there, though that is not clear.

Hitler delayed immediate transportation but approved many other measures suggested by

Goebbels. These included reducing Jewish rations, forcing Jews to wear the Star of David to identify themselves, and taking a census that would make it easier to transport them in the future. Still, Goebbels did not like the fact that Jews remained in Berlin. He continued pushing for their removal and soon got his way.

Around this time, Goebbels met with Reinhard Heydrich. Heydrich was an SS official who played an important role in carrying out the Final Solution. Shortly after their meeting in the fall of 1941, many Berlin Jews were deported to Poland. At first they went to ghettos, special sections of cities where only Jews could live, but soon they were shipped to concentration camps.

Some of these camps were work camps, where Jews were treated as slaves whose lives were expendable. They were like machine parts meant to be used up and discarded. Other camps were extermination camps, where most of those arriving were quickly killed.

In late March 1942, Goebbels dictated a diary entry about the plans for the Final Solution. "Beginning with Lublin," he said, mentioning a Polish town, "Jews ... will be shipped eastward. The procedure is a pretty barbaric one and not to be described here more definitely. Not much will remain of the Jews." "Eastward" was Belzec, a special camp that had opened a week and a half before Goebbels' diary entry. Jews were ushered into a chamber that looked like a spa bath and told

Prisoners arrive at Belzec, one of the first concentration camps to systemically kill its inmates.

to breathe in the purifying air. The air was carbon monoxide.

Zyklon B or prussic acid would soon replace carbon monoxide at Belzec and the other death camps. It was a quicker and more efficient killer. In the coming months, Belzec would be joined by several other camps, each with the capacity to murder tens of thousands of people in a week. Belzec alone would account for six hundred thousand deaths during the war.

CHAPTER SIX

LATTER STAGES OF THE WAR

As the war continued, Goebbels launched a campaign to rally leaders and the people to the realities of the harsh war. In his opinion, German people had not yet begun to make the sacrifices necessary for victory. He realized that people in England and Russia, on the other hand, already had.

Goebbels gave a speech on February 13, 1943, at the Berlin Sportpalast to rally the German people—and the Nazi leadership. He believed that many Germans and especially Nazi leaders were not doing everything they could for the war. He knew that many Nazis lived in luxury, refusing to do without comforts. They refused, in his opinion, to do what was necessary to win the war. He hoped that the recent defeat at Stalingrad would convince people to commit to the war effort.

"Total war is the demand of the hour!" shouted Goebbels as he pushed his face nearly into the microphone. "The danger facing us is enormous. The efforts we take to meet it must be just as enormous. The time has come to remove the gloves and use our fists!" As he shouted into the microphone, Goebbels looked like he was ready to explode. But he was actually very calm and controlled; the emotion was all part of his technique.

Goebbels had a huge crowd of supporters at his February 13, 1943, speech about the need for total war.

Historians today often point to the Russian victory over the Germans at Stalingrad as one of the great turning points of the war. A large portion of the German army was destroyed in the battle. After Stalingrad, the German army was never able to seize the initiative on the eastern front. Still, it was difficult to see how important the battle was at the time.

Goebbels seemed to. He still believed Germany would win, but he worked hard behind the scenes to help mobilize production and increase the size of the armed forces. Though Hitler did not agree to the plans at first, gradually Goebbels won more and more power to mobilize the country. In January 1944, for example, he was appointed president of Berlin. But as the war continued, Goebbels' power had less meaning. Germany was losing: many of its factories had been destroyed, much of its army had been killed, and people were becoming sick of the war. Goebbels' propaganda had less and less influence, though many Germans continued to fight with all their might.

ONGOING MASS MURDER

Despite their losses on the battlefield, the Nazis stepped up their extermination of the Jews. Goebbels' diary entries during 1942 and 1943 show that he knew about the continued slaughter. As Gauleiter of Berlin and an important member of the government, he added directly to this mass murder by constantly pushing for more measures against the Jews. His anti-Semitism was as fanatical as ever.

Publicly, Goebbels linked the Allies with "international Jewry." But he wrote in his diary that he believed that Great Britain and the United States would be pleased by the murder of the Jews. In 1943, he also wrote that Hitler directed him not to leave a single Jew in all of Germany. There are other references to the Final Solution, including some that hint Goebbels understood it was a great crime. For example, he wrote that "there is no going back."

SUPPORTING THE PEOPLE OF BERLIN

British bombers had been attacking Berlin on and off since 1940. In 1943, the nighttime raids stepped up. American daylight raids also began in large numbers. As the Allies grew more powerful, the attacks began to do more and more damage. Civilian houses and apartment buildings as well as factories were destroyed, killing thousands of people.

Goebbels took charge of emergency services, personally directing fire and rescue crews. He helped deliver food and appeared at funerals for civilians killed during the raids. Battered Berliners were grateful for his efforts. He was the only high-ranking Nazi who actually met with people and helped them in the streets.

Wearing a hat with a dark band, Goebbels meets with Berliners who have been displaced by a British raid.

In the summer of 1944, the Americans and British landed in northern France. After heavy fighting, their armies began racing toward Germany. The end was near. As a high-ranking official close to Hitler, Goebbels knew that the war had begun to go badly. Some, including Albert Speer, believed that he realized the war would be lost. Speer was in charge of the German war industry and a close ally and friend of Goebbels. But others are not so sure. Goebbels still had faith in Hitler and believed wholeheartedly in the Nazi revolution. At least at times, he seems to have thought Germany would somehow prevail. So he was shocked when he learned that army leaders had plotted to kill Hitler.

HOLOCAUST REMEMBRANCE

In the decades since World War II ended, Germany has struggled to come to terms with its national responsibility for the Holocaust. More than one hundred thousand Jews now live in Germany, but that is still a sharp decline from the more than half a million Jews who made their home in Germany in 1933, according to census records. Like many other nations, Germany holds Holocaust memorial events every year, often at former concentration camps on the date that prisoners there were freed in 1945.

The Nazis' first concentration camp was set up at Dachau, outside Munich, in 1933. On April 29, 2015, the seventieth anniversary of the camp's liberation, more than 130 survivors and liberators (members of the U.S. Seventh Army's 45th Infantry Division) attended a ceremony there. The president of the Dachau Camp Community, survivor Max Mannheimer, declared, "From commemoration there must also emerge a consciousness of responsibility," according to German international broadcaster Deutsche Welle.

German chancellor Angela Merkel visits the Dachau memorial alongside Max Mannheimer and other survivors.

ATTEMPTED ASSASSINATION

On July 20, 1944, Goebbels was in his Berlin office talking with Speer and another Nazi when the phone rang. He went over to his desk and picked up the phone.

The man on the other line told him a bomb had gone off at the Führer's headquarters in Rastenburg. Hitler, though injured, was still alive. Goebbels put down the phone and told the others what had happened. Then he began criticizing Speer because there was a rumor that one of Speer's workers was part of the plot. This rumor would later turn out to be false, though Goebbels didn't know that at the time.

After dismissing Speer, Goebbels flew into action and soon learned that the attempt was part of a large conspiracy. He mobilized Nazi forces in Berlin and ordered the arrest of one of the main conspirators. He broadcast news of the failed attempt and turned his home into a command post. The rebellion was quickly overcome.

After the failed assassination, Nazi officials examine the damage done to the meeting room of Hitler's headquarters in Rastenburg.

Two days after the assassination attempt, Goebbels met with Hitler. By now the war, stress, and his personal habits had damaged Hitler's health. He seemed pale and old. Others thought he was frail. But Goebbels, still under his spell, felt God had chosen Hitler and preserved him from assassination.

In the wake of the plot, Goebbels was given new authority in the Third Reich. With Speer and Himmler, he closed factories that weren't producing weapons or ammunition. He increased work hours and drafted many people who had been excused from military service earlier.

A last-ditch offensive by German troops in the winter, now known as the Battle of the Bulge, caught the Americans and British off-guard. However, they soon recovered and continued their attack. In the east, the Soviet army steamrolled through Poland into Germany.

Even so, the extermination of the Jews continued. SS units tried removing some of the evidence of the killing camps. In most cases, however, the evidence of so many murders was too obvious to be obliterated.

SUICIDE AND DEFEAT

On April 21, 1945, Goebbels sat at his office in Berlin and prepared a radio speech. As he urged Berliners to fight without mercy, a Russian artillery shell landed outside. The window blew in, sending glass and wood flying everywhere, yet Goebbels calmly continued his speech.

By the end of April 1945, it was clear that the Third Reich's time could be counted in days, not weeks or years. The day after he recorded the speech, Goebbels and his family left their home to join the Führer. Hitler was in a bunker complex in the Chancellery garden near the center of Berlin. Two long flights of stairs downward led to a corridor and a suite of twelve rooms in the upper bunker. Another part of the bunker housed an SS guard unit. The Führerbunker, Hitler's headquarters and living area, was down another twelve steps. The Goebbels family moved in with him.

The air was stuffy. The ventilating system whined constantly. But there was more than twelve feet of concrete protecting the ceiling, plus another thirty feet between the ceiling and the surface—necessary protection against bombs and artillery.

Hitler's health had broken over the past six months. He had the symptoms of Parkinson's disease and depended on injections of vitamins and caffeine. Hitler and others talked about miracles, but there was little doubt the end was near. Goebbels may have persuaded Hitler to make his last stand in the capital.

At 3 p.m. on April 30, Hitler bit down on a cyanide capsule. At the same moment, he pulled the trigger on his Walther pistol. He wanted no possibility that he would survive.

Hitler's body was taken upstairs into the garden. A shallow grave was dug. The corpse was laid together with that of Eva Braun. She had been Hitler's mistress; they had married only the day before. She, too, had committed suicide. Several cans of gasoline were poured over their remains, and Hitler's aides saluted as the flames leaped from the ground.

Hitler had appointed Goebbels chancellor, but there was nothing Goebbels could do at this point to prevent Germany's defeat. He knew that the Allies would execute him if he was captured. As the Russian troops closed in on the afternoon of May 1, 1945, he and his wife said good-bye to the others in the bunker. Magda and a doctor gave morphine injections to the six Goebbels children, putting them to sleep in their bunk beds. She then broke cyanide capsules in their mouths.

The sounds of the approaching Russian army could

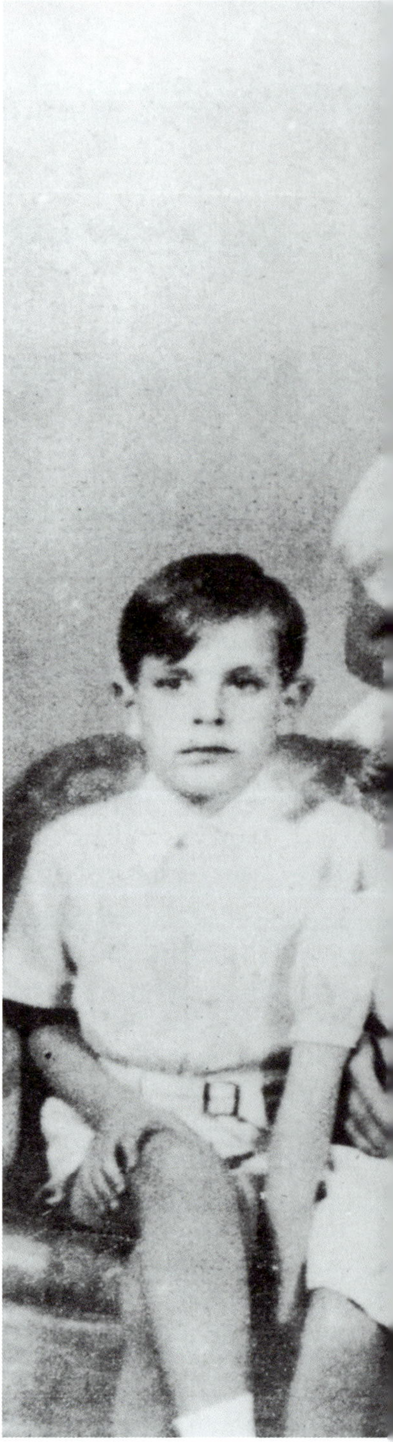

Goebbels' stepson, Harald Quandt, was added to this 1942 photo of the family. He was the only one of them to survive the war.

be heard above. It was now about 8:30 p.m. Goebbels made his assistant promise to burn his and his family's bodies. Then he and his wife closed the door. There was a gunshot. When his assistant opened the door, both of the Goebbels were dead. Both had taken cyanide; Goebbels had also shot himself in the head, like his leader.

An SS man fired once into each of the dead bodies to make sure they were truly dead. Then the aide took the bodies up to the garden and burned them, as he had promised.

CHAPTER SEVEN

LESSONS AND LEGACY OF GOEBBELS' PROPAGANDA

To the very end, Goebbels railed against Jews, spewing venom in his speeches and writings. Some have theorized that his hatred for Jews was motivated by politics. But the sheer volume of his evil words demands further explanation. It seems true that at times he pushed for persecution of the Jews for political reasons. He knew this would influence many Germans and that supporting virulent anti-Semitism would win Hitler's favor.

It also seems obvious that Goebbels truly hated Jews. This hate may have grown over time, but by the time he was a government official it must have been genuine. It was emotional, and it was intellectual. In some instances, Goebbels seems to have been willing to tolerate people whose ancestors included Jews as well as non-Jews. However,

Jud Süss, which depicted a conniving Jewish businessman who is eventually executed, was one of the Nazis' most infamous anti-Semitic propaganda films.

ultimately he saw Jews as an inferior race that stood in the way of the Nazi revolution. They were therefore the enemy, and he hated all enemies.

When he spoke of Hitler as Führer—even as a god—Goebbels was sincere. He believed in the myth of the master race that he helped spread. To him, this vision of the Führer was more than a myth. He believed a new age was coming, and he placed all of his intellectual talents and energy in the service of the Nazi revolution.

The revolution required the elimination of the Jews. So the man who showed mercy to the bombed-out victims of Berlin thought nothing of paving the way for the murder of millions of others whose only crime was having a different heritage than his. He did not recognize the evil of his actions; on the contrary, he thought his actions were the opposite of evil. Those who thought such actions were a crime were, by his thinking, members of the old civilization, which had to be destroyed.

Goebbels and the Nazis saw themselves at the forefront of an important historical movement. That belief colored everything they saw and did. Exterminating the Jews, by Hitler's logic, would set the stage for a great Germany that would last for a thousand years.

Goebbels' youthful search for God led him to the devil instead. More than six million people died as a result. But, of course, Goebbels did not act alone; many, many others shared his guilt.

THE POWER OF PROPAGANDA

Joseph Goebbels is certainly not alone in his use of propaganda to persuade people. Other nations, including the United States and the United Kingdom, had similar campaigns during World War II to get people to support the war effort. American propaganda exaggerated military victories, downplayed losses, and disparaged their enemies, just as Goebbels' ministry did. Whereas the Nazis focused on Jews, a major theme of American posters and films was the threat of the Japanese, who were portrayed as cruel and ruthless barbarians who would use any means necessary to build their empire.

However, one important difference is that Goebbels had almost complete control of all the media in Nazi Germany. Other dictatorships have also found great success in using propaganda to their advantage. For example, in 1966 Mao Zedong launched the Cultural Revolution to suppress all opposition to his communist regime in China. In nations with democratic governments, other viewpoints are available in addition to the government's, although the freedom of the press is sometimes restricted during wartime or for other reasons related to national security.

ASSESSING WHO IS TO BLAME

Much of the work done by Goebbels and his team might be compared to what advertising agencies or political campaign managers do today, using various tactics to convince the public to buy certain products or agree with one party's positions. We despise the Nazis' goals as well as their distortions of truth and history. But we must also recognize that their methods are familiar to us—and effective.

We should also recognize that Goebbels could not have succeeded in creating the Hitler myth without the support of the German people. His ravings against the Jews could not have gone largely unchallenged without at least some of the people in the audience agreeing with him.

"While recognizing the abilities of the Nazi propaganda lords," wrote one of the American prosecutors at the Nuremberg war trials, "I cannot recognize or accept the premise, so often advanced, that the German people could do nothing about it. Having spent nearly three years in Nuremberg poring over historical documents and interrogating and crossexamining hundreds of witness ... I became convinced of the collective guilt of the German people for the dastardly crimes visited upon the members of the Jewish

Goebbels was instrumental in creating the ideal of "One Nation, One Empire, One Leader," as seen in a banner at a Sportpalast speech he gave in 1938.

faith. Normally, I believe guilt to be an individual matter ... In the case of the German crimes, however, I must reverse my entire philosophy and conclude that only by collective guilt of the German people could this nightmare of history ever have taken place."

And if the German people of the 1920s, '30s, and '40s could agree with hateful propaganda, so could we.

THE LAST BELIEVER

As the war wound down, most Germans realized that the core of Goebbels' propaganda was misleading and false. Few believed in the myth of the "superman" or Nazi revolution any longer.

One man, however, remained a true believer to the very end: Goebbels. Still blaming "international Jewry" for the Nazis' collapse, he saw greatness where others saw only evil. "Do not let yourself be disconcerted by the worldwide clamor that will now begin," Goebbels wrote in his last letter to his stepson. "One day the lies will crumble away of themselves and truth will triumph once more."

If he was correct, it was not in the way he supposed.

TIMELINE

1897 Paul Joseph Goebbels born in Rheydt, Germany, on October 29.

1907 A desperate operation on Goebbels' foot fails, leaving him permanently disabled.

1914–1918 World War I. Goebbels' clubfoot prevents him from joining the army, but he does civilian service in support of the war effort.

1921 Goebbels gets his Ph.D. Despite his education, he has difficulty finding a job because of the hard economic times in Germany.

1924 Goebbels joins the Nazi movement.

1925 Goebbels meets Hitler for the first time. Already known as an inflammatory speaker, Goebbels rises quickly in the small party.

1926 Hitler appoints Goebbels Gauleiter of Berlin. He is charged with reorganizing and revitalizing the local party. He reshapes the local SA, using it for violent demonstrations. His methods include violence, fanatical anti-Semitism, and relentless attacks on his enemies.

1928 Goebbels is elected to the Reichstag, despite the Nazi Party's poor showing in the election overall.

1931 Goebbels marries Magda Quandt, a divorcée with a ten-year-old son named

Harald. Together, the Goebbels have six other children.

1932 Goebbels helps convince Hitler to run for president. Though Hitler loses, the election cements the Party's importance in German politics. The Nazis do well enough in the year's parliamentary elections to dominate the Reichstag.

1933 Adolf Hitler becomes chancellor of Germany. Goebbels is appointed minister of propaganda and culture in March and immediately begins crackdowns on Jewish newspapers.

1935 The Nuremberg Laws are passed, legalizing discrimination against Jews.

1938 Goebbels helps organize Kristallnacht, or the Night of Broken Glass. Jews all across Germany are beaten, robbed, and killed. Meanwhile, Germans troops enter Austria, taking over the country. In October, they occupy the Sudetenland in Czechoslovakia.

1939 Germany invades Poland on September 1. Poland falls before the end of the month. After visiting Poland, Goebbels discusses the "Jewish question" with Hitler and pushes for the removal of Jews from Germany.

1940 Germany invades France, Belgium, Holland, and Luxembourg.

1941 Germany invades the Soviet Union.

1943 The tide of the war begins to turn. Goebbels uses the German defeat at Stalingrad to argue for increased war mobilization. He wants Nazi Party leaders, as well as the common people, to make more sacrifices. Meanwhile, he becomes a familiar visitor to bombed-out areas of Berlin, where victims of Allied bombing welcome him. Thousands, and then millions, of Jews are executed in the death camps.

1944 Goebbels is given more emergency powers. The outcome of the war appears inevitable as Russia threatens Germany's borders and the Americans and British land in France. The Holocaust continues.

1945 The Allies close in on Germany. With Russian troops only a few blocks away, Hitler and Goebbels commit suicide in Berlin. The Holocaust finally ends.

GLOSSARY

adherent Supporter of a certain political party or other set of ideas.

anti-Semitism Hatred of Jews; one of the prime causes of the rise of the Nazis and the Holocaust. Unfortunately, anti-Semitism has a long history throughout the world and remains a problem to this day.

bourgeoisie The rich and middle class who own most property, wealth, and industry in society.

carnage Slaughter or massacre; mass murder.

censorship The suppression of objectionable books or other materials.

concentration camp General term for special prison compounds used by Nazis and overseen by the SS. Besides Jews, political prisoners, prisoners of war, Roma (gypsies), and homosexuals were among those imprisoned or killed in such camps during World War II.

denounce To publicly condemn or verbally attack.

exorbitant Excessive, as in a price that is unreasonably high.

faction A small group within a larger organization, often used in reference to opposing political parties in a government.

Final Solution The term adopted by the Nazi government for the plan to kill all Jews in Europe. Sometimes historians use the term to note the contrast with earlier stages of Nazi thinking, which may have allowed for "merely" removing Jews from Europe and not necessarily killing all of them. This plan was sometimes called "Madagascar," after the island that was the supposed destination.

Führer German word for "leader"; Hitler's title while he was dictator of Germany.

Gau A local Nazi district or organization.

Gauleiter The head of the Gau. Goebbels was appointed Gauleiter of Berlin in 1926.

Gentile A non-Jew.

ghetto A general term for any area of a city set aside for a certain group of people. Jews lived in ghettos throughout much of European history. Laws restricting ghettos and activities there have varied greatly over time. During World War II, the Germans established ghettos in occupied countries to help prepare for the elimination of Jews.

instigate To start or stir up trouble.

reparations Payment that a defeated state is forced to pay to a victorious state for damage done during a war.

rhetorical Of or relating to rhetoric, the art of persuasive public speaking or writing.

SA The Sturmabteilung, or "storm detachment." Also known as the Brownshirts. Nazi Party organization that helped Hitler and Goebbels. The SA was a kind of private army often used to intimidate enemies and fight with the police and Communists. Brownshirts also attacked Jews.

scapegoat A person or group forced to take the blame for something.

SS The Schutzstaffel, or guard unit of the Nazi Party. Members swore personal allegiance to Adolf Hitler. This massive organization swelled to over one million members during the war.

Star of David A six-pointed star often used as a religious symbol. Nazi laws required Jews to wear a Star of David at all times in the occupied territories, and later in Germany.

virulent Very harmful in its effects.

FOR MORE INFORMATION

Canadian Human Rights Museum
85 Israel Asper Way
Winnipeg, MB R3C 0L
Canada
(204) 289-2000
Website: http://humanrights.ca
The Canadian Human Rights Museum is dedicated to making a difference in people's lives by providing a center for learning and research about human rights.

Canadian National Holocaust Monument
Corner of Wellington and Booth Streets
Ottawa, ON K1A 0M8
Canada
Website: http://www.holocaustmonument.ca
Canada, the only Allied nation without a Holocaust memorial monument in its capital, is building a monument to remember the Holocaust and celebrate the forty thousand Holocaust survivors who live in Canada. The monument will be across the street from the Canadian War Museum in Ottawa.

The Jewish Museum
1109 5th Avenue

New York, NY 10128
(212) 423-3200
Website: http://thejewishmuseum.org
Founded in 1904, the Jewish Museum is the oldest museum devoted to Jewish art and culture. It offers programs and exhibitions for people of all ages and backgrounds

Museum of Tolerance
Simon Wiesenthal Plaza
9786 West Pico Boulevard
Los Angeles, CA 90035
(310) 553-8403
Website: http://www.museumoftolerance.org
The Museum of Tolerance focuses on the Holocaust as well as more contemporary prejudice and discrimination around the world.

United States Holocaust Memorial Museum
100 Raoul Wallenberg Place, SW
Washington, D.C. 20024-2126
(202) 488-0400
Website: http://www.ushmm.org
Opened in 1993, the United States Holocaust Memorial Museum celebrates the memory of Holocaust victims and teaches visitors about the tragedy and its moral implications. Its website has extensive educational resources for students, teachers, and researchers.

Yad Vashem
The Holocaust Martyrs' and Heroes' Remembrance Authority
P.O. Box 3477
Jerusalem 9103401
Israel
972-2-6443574
Website: http://www.yadvashem.org
Yad Vashem is a living memorial for commemoration, research, education, and documentation of the Holocaust. In addition to its museums in Jerusalem, it provides lists of victims, photos, and other extensive digital archives on its website, as well as educational materials and seminars.

WEBSITES

Because of the changing nature of Internet links, Rosen Publishing has developed an online list of websites related to the subject of this book. This site is updated regularly. Please use this link to access this list:

http://www.rosenlinks.com/HOLO/Goeb

FOR FURTHER READING

Altman, Linda Jacobs. *Hitler, Goebbels, Himmler: The Nazi Holocaust Masterminds* (Remembering the Holocaust). Berkeley Heights, NJ: Enslow Publishers, 2014.

Aly, Götz. *Why the Germans? Why the Jews? Envy, Race Hatred, and the Prehistory of the Holocaust*. Translated by Jefferson Chase. New York, NY: Metropolitan Books, 2011.

Brezina, Corona. *Nazi Architects of the Holocaust* (A Documentary History of the Holocaust). New York, NY: Rosen Publishing, 2014.

Byers, Ann. *Kristallnacht and Living in Nazi Germany* (A Documentary History of the Holocaust). New York, NY: Rosen Publishing, 2014.

Deem, James. *Kristallnacht: The Nazi Terror that Began the Holocaust* (The Holocaust Through Primary Sources). Berkeley Heights, NJ: Enslow Publishers, 2013.

Ellis, Catherine, and Jeremy Roberts. *Adolf Hitler* (The Holocaust). New York, NY: Rosen Publishing, 2015.

Freeman, Charles. *Why Did the Rise of the Nazis Happen?* (Moments in History). New York, NY: Gareth Stevens Publishing, 2010.

Kempowski, Walter. *Swansong 1945: A Collective Diary of the Last Days of the Third Reich.* New York, NY: W.W. Norton, 2015.

Langley, Andrew. *Kristallnacht and Hitler* (Days of Decision). Oxford, England: Raintree, 2014.

Longerich, Peter. *Goebbels: A Biography*. Translated by Alan Bance, Jeremy Noakes, and Lesley Sharpe. New York, NY: Random House, 2015.

Manvell, Roger, and Heinrich Fraenkel. *Doctor Goebbels: His Life and Death*. New York, NY: Skyhorse Publishing, 2010.

Riess, Curt. *Joseph Goebbels*. Charleston, SC: Fonthill Media, 2015.

Schreiber, Mordecai. E*xplaining the Holocaust*. Eugene, OR: Cascade Books, 2015.

Stanley, Jason. *How Propaganda Works*. Princeton, NJ: Princeton University Press, 2015.

Stille, Darlene R. *Architects of the Holocaust*. Mankato, MN: Compass Point Books, 2011.

INDEX

W

ABOUT THE AUTHORS

Kelly Roscoe began investigating the perpetrators of the Holocaust after her first visit to the United States Holocaust Memorial Museum. Born in Vermont's Northeast Kingdom, she now lives and writes in Maine.

Jeremy Roberts has written several biographies for young people, including works on Joan of Arc and Oskar Schindler.

PHOTO CREDITS

Cover, pp. 32-33, 56-57 Keystone-France/Gammy-Keystone/Getty Images; p. 5 Ryan Donnell/Aurora//Getty Images; pp. 6-7 (background) Ingo Jezier-skiPhotographer's Choice/Getty Images; pp. 7 (inset), 52-53 Imagno/Hulton Archive/Getty Images; pp. 9, 19, 27, 45, 60, 74, 89 Rolf E. Staerk/ Shutterstock.com; pp. 10, 42-43 FPG/Archive Photos/Getty Images; pp. 14-15, 17, 20, 61, 78-79, 82-83 ullstein bild/Getty Images; p. 23 Hulton Archive/Getty Images; pp. 24-25 United States Holocaust Memorial Museum, courtesy of Bud Tullin; p. 29 Photo 12/Universal Images Group/Getty Images; pp. 38-39 Roger Viollet/ Getty Images; p. 41 Henry Guttmann/Hulton Archive/Getty Images; pp. 48-49 Universal Images Group/Getty Images; pp. 54-55 Johannes Eisele/AFP/Getty Images; pp. 68-69, 75, 94-95 © AP Images; p. 72 United States Holocaust Memorial Museum; pp. 80-81 Joerg Koch/Getty Images; pp. 86-87 Keystone/ Hulton Archive/Getty Images; p. 90 Galerie Bilderwelt/Hulton Archive/Getty Images; interior pages background textures and graphics Aleksandr Bryliaev/ Shutterstock.com, kak2s/Shutterstock.com, argus/Shutterstock.com, Sfio Cra-cho/Shutterstock.com; back cover Ventura/Shutterstock.com.

Designer: Michael Moy; Editor: Meredith Day;

Photo Researcher: Bruce Donolla